# HOW TO
# DESIGN & MAKE
# WOOD RELIEFS

## Robert Skinner

Art Department, Southampton College of Long Island University

Dover Publications, Inc.
New York

Published in Canada by General Publishing Company, Ltd., 30 Lesmill Road, Don Mills, Toronto, Ontario.
Published in the United Kingdom by Constable and Company, Ltd., 10 Orange Street, London WC2H 7EG.

*How to Design and Make Wood Reliefs* is a new work, first published by Dover Publications, Inc., in 1980.

*International Standard Book Number: 0-486-24057-6*
*Library of Congress Catalog Card Number: 80-66960*

Manufactured in the United States of America
Dover Publications, Inc.
180 Varick Street
New York, N.Y. 10014

# CONTENTS

# Introduction:
# Reliefs and Their History

A relief is a picture or design that is carved, worked, cast or constructed, in any material, above or below the surface that surrounds it. When it stands so far out from the surrounding surface as to seem almost separate from it, it is called a high relief. A shallow relief, barely raised from the surface, is called a low relief, or bas-relief.

Man's desire to make sculptured reliefs is as old as man himself. Among the famous cave paintings in France are also found reliefs of animals and women carved into the rock walls. In most cases the sculptor took advantage of (or perhaps was inspired by) rock outcroppings and bulges in the flat wall, reshaping them into whatever animal image the outcropping suggested.

For almost three thousand years the Egyptians carved or worked endless reliefs and millions of hieroglyphs in stone, wood, clay, gold and other metals, most made to celebrate the grandeur of the then-reigning Pharaoh. They range in size from tiny images in precious stone to monumental representations of the Pharaoh several stories high. Such a volume of work led Egyptians to the invention of the sunken or incised relief (Fig. 1), in

**Fig. 2.** Detail of the Panathenaean Procession frieze from the Parthenon in Athens (stone carving).

which a shallow image was cut into a smooth, flat surface without carving away any of the surrounding material. They also learned very early that the illusion of considerable depth in a very shallow relief could be achieved by overlapping. that is, by carving outlines of objects next to each other in a way that made them appear to be one behind the other.

Although the Egyptians mastered various techniques of relief carving, it was the Greeks who developed the relief fully for decorative and narrative purposes. In the Panathenaean Procession that once adorned the Parthenon (Fig. 2), the sensitivity of the relief carving is such that the figures seem more real than those carved fully in the round for the same building. During this "golden age" of Greece (especially the fifth and fourth centuries B.C.), sculptors were even able to create the illusion of diaphanous gowns on the maidens in their carved reliefs. The Romans so enjoyed the relief as an art form that the Column of Trajan (113 A.D.), to take just one example, was carved with a spiral relief over 650 feet long. By the third century A.D., however, quality had sadly declined.

The sculptured relief achieved major importance again during the great wave of cathedral building in the Gothic period (Fig. 3) and during the Renaissance that

**Fig. 1.** Egyptian incised relief (stone carving).

**Fig. 3.** Portal sculpture from a Gothic cathedral (stone carving).

followed, that is, from the twelfth through the sixteenth centuries. The volume of architectural, decorative and illusionistic relief on the great churches, from Italy to England, has not been exceeded by any other age or culture.

With the development of oil paints during the Renaissance and the subsequent popularity of two-dimensional illusionistic painting, relief sculpture declined in favor. It has not been until the twentieth century that the relief—now the relief construction—has found expression again as a popular technique among artists.

While many great sculptors of the past hundred years have contributed to the modern relief, it is to Pablo Picasso, Jean Arp and Louise Nevelson that most attention should be given.

Picasso's importance comes not so much from the number of reliefs he made, but from his creation, in 1912, along with Georges Braque, of the first collages. Collage, the art of pasting paper and other materials onto a flat surface, led quickly to assemblage, the art of building out from a surface in relief or in the round, often with found objects. It is assemblage that has been the major form of sculptural relief in our time.

Two characteristics emerge in most assemblage: the use largely of found objects in the work, and the constructing or building up of the work, usually from a flat surface. Both of these characteristics are peculiar to the twentieth century because in no culture before our own has such a wealth of new and discarded material been available for the artist to use (an indication of the degree to which a culture influences its own art). Further, in no other culture has the sculptor been sufficiently free from tradition to construct—that is, to build by adding elements—rather than to de-struct, that is, to carve away or subtract from the material. Before 1912 sculpture was made in only three ways: by carving (stone or wood), by casting (in bronze) or by repoussé (shaping thin metal from the back, a relief process). Certainly there were, and are, other processes such as the shaping of clay, wax or plaster, and casting in concrete, steel and aluminum, but these are essentially preliminary to or related to the major methods.

Picasso's first assemblages, or constructions (the words are often used interchangeably), followed his first collages almost immediately. His *Guitar* (Fig. 4) of sheet metal and wire was made in 1912 (and another very similar to it in 1924), and a construction of painted wood called *Musical Instruments* was made in 1914. In both, the emphasis on the space within and around the piece is at least as strong as the emphasis on the mass. Or, to put it other ways, the voids are as important as

**Fig. 4.** *Guitar*, 1912, by Pablo Picasso, an assemblage of metal and wire. (Collection of The Museum of Modern Art, New York)

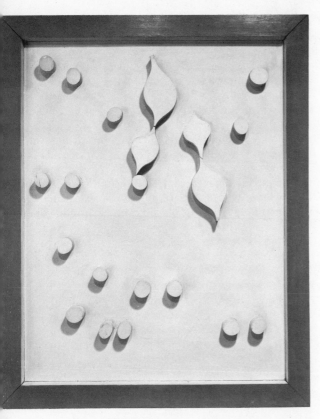

Fig. 5. *Leaves and Navels, I*, 1930, by Jean Arp, a painted wood relief. (Collection of The Museum of Modern Art, New York)

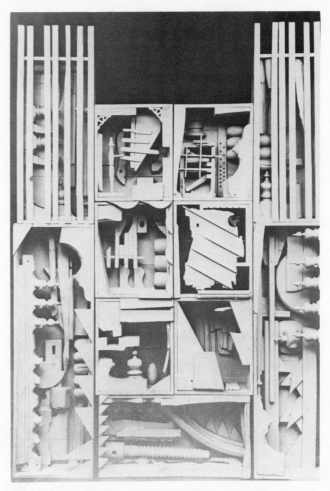

Fig. 6. *Dawn's Wedding Chapel*, 1968, by Louise Nevelson, a painted wood relief.

the solids, or the negative areas are as important as the positive areas. This concept had emerged in Impressionist painting a few years earlier, when interest in subject matter began to be replaced with more interest in form. This trend grew, to culminate, at about the same time, in the style known as abstraction.

Picasso's reliefs were soon followed by those of Jean Arp. After several collages in 1915, Arp produced his first wood relief in 1916. For the next 16 years his major works were wood reliefs, most made of new material and many painted in bright colors (Fig. 5). Later ones were more often painted white or black or simply varnished. His shapes were simple abstractions drawn freely without conscious representation of particular objects. Once they were completed, he called them whatever he thought they looked like in nature.

Louise Nevelson has become one of the best-known and most respected sculptors of our time through her development of the relief assemblage made of found wood. Since the early 1940s she has constructed hundreds of reliefs and free-standing pieces out of wood salvaged from demolished buildings and dismantled factories, millwork waste and furniture of all kinds. She is best known for her boxes: deep reliefs built within discarded crates and boxes of all shapes and sizes assembled together to cover entire walls and fill large rooms (Fig. 6). Most of her work is painted totally in a rich velvety black, although she has occasionally made completely white and completely gold assemblages. A desire for weather-proof sculpture has sometimes led her to the use of plastics, Cor-ten steel and cast bronze, but Nevelson has always returned to wood, and essentially to the relief, as her principal medium and technique.

# Section 1

# FREE-FORM WOOD RELIEFS

# 1

# Analysis of a Free-Form Relief: "Early Forms"

Before plunging ahead to make your first relief, you should consider several elements of the design. By analyzing the first relief in this book you will gain an understanding of what went into its planning that may help to make yours a successful piece.

The total concept for *Early Forms* (Fig. 7) came from a fondness for simple, even primitive, shapes, together with a respect for the way puzzles fit together. Several line drawings of shapes in various arrangements were made on scrap paper before deciding on this one. Full-scale paper patterns were then cut out, trimmed, changed and arranged before transferring the patterns to wood. In addition to the integrated arrangement of interesting shapes, there had to be variety among the shapes to avoid repetition and boredom, and unity within the arrangement to "hold it together" (variety and unity, you will note, are also essential to life and work as well).

The shapes range from very basic (the egg and the circles) to suggestive (a spoon? a fork? a tool?) to nonrepresentational and new shapes. Relationships of shapes within any design are important to its unity. In this relief seven circles relate immediately to one another even though they exhibit differences in size, color, grain pattern and texture. They relate also to the one egg shape, and to the round hole. There is (or should be!) a conscious or subconscious effort by the observer to find the circle that came from the hole. This positive-negative relationship of circle to hole is reinforced by another shape with an interior hole and the shape that came from it, even though the holes are completely different. Another shape relationship is found among the pieces that partially enclose another piece, such as those enclosing the "spoon" (right of center) and the "egg" (upper left-hand corner). Similar but more shallow enclosures occur at top center and in the lower row of pieces.

Relationships among shapes are the most quickly perceived but relationships of texture, size, value (the amount of black or white in an object) and grain pattern can also be found.

We have already spoken of the positive-negative contrasts found in early twentieth-century reliefs. Such contrast creates tension and gives "life" to a work of art,

and should be a consideration in the designing of sculptural reliefs. Contrast can be created in several ways: as a play between mass and space (solids and voids), as a play between light and shadow (mass causes shadows depending on the amount and source of light), as a play between light and dark surfaces (tone or color) and as a play between smooth and rough surfaces (texture). All of these contrasting elements, and more, exist in any work of art, and the degree to which they have been considered by the artist is often the degree to which the work is successful.

Continuing our analysis of *Early Forms*, we will look at each of these positive-negative contrasts. The play between mass and space (the wooden shapes and the space around them) is perhaps most dynamic where S-curves occur and where space suddenly changes direction. These areas can be found in the lower right quarter, the upper left center, the lower left corner and the center. The areas of more vertical and unchanging direction are more static and less interesting. Where much space surrounds a wood shape (far right center), the "space shape" is lost and, with it, some of the interest.

The play between light and shadow in *Early Forms* is difficult to see in a photograph, since the observer's point of view cannot change in this case. The particular lighting in this photo was chosen in order to show the wooden shapes as three-dimensional. If the relief had been lit from all sides and the front, shadows would have disappeared and the relief would have looked totally flat. Much is lost in a photograph of sculpture which was made to be seen in three dimensions and which relies partially on light and shadow changes for its effect.

The play of light and dark is more apparent here than the play of light and shadow. Values range from three very light-colored pieces to three very dark pieces. Between these extremes are about four shades of brown (gray in the photograph). These contrasts are subtle and transitional rather than bold and sudden. Contrasts may be subtle or bold in a work of art, although art that relies solely on extreme and sudden contrasts for excitement is often not interesting over a long period. Within some of the pieces the wood-grain pattern, weathering

Fig. 7. *Early Forms*, a wood relief by the author.

tones and cracks create light-and-dark play as well. Four or five pieces in the relief have very distinct grain patterns. The rest vary from an almost imperceptible pattern to a slight pattern. Again, it is the range and variety of contrasts, both subtle and sudden between extremes, that help determine the interest of a work.

The play of texture between smooth and rough surfaces is related to the variety of grain patterns. The difference is that texture is actually smooth or rough while grain pattern only looks smooth or rough. We are apt to associate a fine, barely perceptible grain pattern with smoothness and a bold grain pattern with roughness. We know, however, that this association is not necessarily true. In planning and selecting wood for a relief, the play between rough and smooth textures can become interestingly complex. This can be seen more readily in the relief *Wheels* (see Fig. 11), where two parts of the same piece of wood are used smooth and rough as they become elements of a circle or elements of a rectangle.

# 2

# Making a Free-Form Wood Relief: "Integral"

The only way to start your relief is by collecting wood. The more stock you have at hand to select from, the easier it is to combine interesting pieces. In collecting planks and boards, look for variety in grain pattern, color, size, thickness and texture. New wood and building plywood are the least interesting for a wood relief, although new wood can be used for contrast sometimes and can be picked up from scrap at construction sites and millwork shops. Barn boards in all stages of wear and decay are particularly desirable. Pallets and industrial crating can be found everywhere, from urban manufacturing plants to rural farm warehouses. Dumps and landfill areas are gold mines to the sculptor who works with found material. Beaches, bays, riverbanks, and shorelines are continuous sources of flotsam. The stockpile will grow quickly if you are continually on the lookout for wood, picking it up when you find it, even though it may be dirty, wet or of questionable value to you at the time. In these days of energy consciousness and a trend toward wood-burning stoves, you are apt to encounter competition in your search for wood.

Clean the pieces when they have dried (Fig. 8). A wide wire brush will not damage fragile old boards yet will easily remove embedded dirt and flaking paint. Wood that is actually rotting around knot and nail holes should be cleaned vigorously to remove all the rotten material. Such pieces often have considerable character but must be handled with care. Brush pieces only in the direction of the grain. A wire brush wheel on your power drill will quickly wear depressions in any wood surface and should not be used. A variety of tools is available for removing nails: a claw and rip hammer, a pinch bar with nail slot and claw, and a cat's-paw. All of these tools should be used with a large, flat scrap of wood as a fulcrum for leverage and as a pad to protect the surface from tool marks. Where nails cannot be pulled easily, they may be driven out from the back with a nail set, or broken off in the wood. Unscarred nail holes and the natural marks of wear and decay can enhance a relief, but artificially made distress marks usually look as fake as they are.

If wood must be stored out of doors, it is best stacked vertically and loosely in a corner where it can't be blown over. Sun and rain will continue to change exposed surface color, although not appreciably unless the wood is exposed for many months.

If you have worked with wood extensively, you are already aware of its limitations. If you are just beginning to work with wood, you'll have to learn what it will do and won't do. Thin necks or narrow bridges across the grain will break easily, particularly in old wood. Try to avoid them in designing your own reliefs. Tight knots may be featured in a shape rather than cut through. Not only is a knot likely to loosen and fall out if cut through; the presence of a cut knot indicates that the sculptor is somewhat insensitive to his material.

To begin the relief *Integral*, study the photo of the completed work (Fig. 9) and the diagram of lettered template pieces (Fig. 10). The actual templates, with the corresponding letters, will be found in the heavy-paper section of this book. Cut out the templates and place the larger ones on a few pieces of your collected boards. The long axis of the shape should correspond with the grain of the wood. Try each of the large templates on several boards until you have found the area of a board that is most compatible with the shape. Use knots, nail holes or other unusual features sparingly within a

Fig. 8. Tools useful for cleaning wood.

Fig. 9. The completed relief *Integral*.

couple of shapes. Avoid taking shapes from the same board that will be next to each other in the finished relief. Use from four to six different boards selected for their contrasting colors, grains, thicknesses and textures. Both texture and color can be altered by sanding the faces of some pieces after they have been cut out. This will reveal light, fresh color beneath a weather-stained or worn surface. As you continue to lay out the remaining templates, refer frequently to the photo of the finished relief to assure that there will be a variety of relationships and contrasts. No area of the relief should dominate attention but all areas should command some interest.

Tack the templates in place with push-pins and draw around the larger ones on the boards with a soft-lead pencil. Remove the templates and cut out each shape with a saber saw or band saw. (On particularly fragile wood the shoe of the saber saw will crush ridges and leave marks that cannot be taken out. To prevent this, clamp a thin sheet of pressed board such as Masonite over the wooden board and cut both at once.) As each piece is cut out, lay it in its relative position on a full-scale sheet of cardboard. Using this care throughout

construction will help avoid mix-ups and damage. Continue to cut out the rest of the shapes. Where necessary, pencil marks can be erased and the cut edges sanded on a belt sander, sanding wheel or block.

At this point the box frame must be made (see Section IV).

If your shapes have been cut from found wood, they are undoubtedly of different thicknesses, a factor you considered in selecting the boards. They do not need to be mounted at different heights from the backboard unless still greater height contrast is desired. In either case, shapes should not be raised so far from the backboard that they protrude above the depth of the frame or reveal the posts on which they are mounted. A ½" or ¾" space between the pieces and the backboard is enough to give the pieces a floating quality.

Posts should be set about ¼" into the pieces and into the backboard, so posts of 1" or 1¼" in length should be cut from a ¼" dowel. Plan on two posts for most pieces, three for the largest pieces and one post for only the smallest pieces. Bore ¼" holes ¼" deep into the back of each piece, locating the holes near each end of the center axis to keep the posts from being seen. A drill

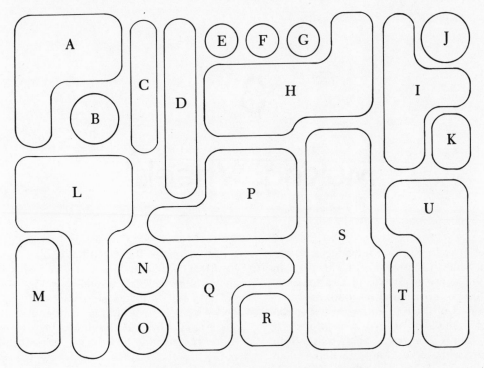

**Fig. 10.** Diagram of the templates for *Integral*.

ress with a depth stop is best for truly aligned holes, but a hand or power drill can be used. A piece of masking tape around the drill bit serves well as a depth gauge. If the wood is fragile, the hole may have to be bored deeper (and a longer post may have to be cut). Before tapping the post into its hole, squeeze a little wood glue into the hole for permanence. Lay each piece on a padded block when mounting posts to avoid marring the face.

Locating the holes for the posts in the backboard is apt to be the most difficult step of the construction. Start with corner pieces. Place small scrapwood "spacers" against the box-frame walls. (Quarter-inch plywood scraps cut into 2"-by-4" pieces are very useful in any shop as wedges, clamp pads and, here, as spacers.) When the spacers are in place, brush a thin layer of colored paint on the ends of the posts of the corner piece. Position the piece precisely within the spacers

and press it down against the backboard. Paint marks will be left where you must drill for the posts. Use a hand or power drill with masking tape around the bit as a depth gauge. For maximum accuracy, put the bit directly in the center of the paint mark and press down gently before pulling the drill trigger. Squeeze a bit of glue into each hole and tap the piece lightly into its holes with a rubber mallet. Continue to mount pieces in a logical order, working from the outside toward the center, and from the larger pieces to the smaller. Where holes are slightly off, whittle the end of the post a bit to correct the alignment. Absolute precision is not necessary, of course, but spaces should not vary so much as to be disturbing or appear to be mistakes. Pieces can be trimmed if spacing seems crowded, or a new piece or two can be cut if too much space is left as you get to the last pieces. When all the pieces are mounted and the glue is dry, your first relief is done.

# 3

# Making "Wheels"

The wood relief *Wheels* (Fig. 11) introduces at least four elements not found in either *Early Forms* or *Integral*. First, the shapes are geometric (circles, arcs, rectangles) rather than nature-related. Second, each rectangle also forms part of a circle (or two circles); conversely, each circle is made up of three or four pieces of rectangles. This totally integrates the composition: circles do not exist without rectangles to make them; rectangles rely on the circles to relate them. Third, the shapes resulting from the cut rectangles form a pattern of their own distinct from the circles they surround. Finally, there is an element of discovery in the realization that one of the pieces is not a rectangle but is L-shaped. These new design elements, added to the relationships discussed in the earlier chapters, create a totally unified work relying on the actual integration of forms, yet made up of diverse and contrasting forms for variety.

Making this relief of geometric shapes demands more care in marking, cutting and positioning the pieces than in the first reliefs. Since the circles are obviously intended to be perfectly round, they must be marked and cut perfectly round. Likewise, the rectangles must have 90° corners and parallel sides.

To begin, make a box frame with inside measurements between 18″ and 24″ wide and 24″ to 30″ long (see Section IV). Making the frame first will assure you of an accurately finished relief.

Next, select short lengths of board from your stockpile, choosing them for their relationships and contrasts of color, texture, thickness, width and grain pattern. It is wise to begin with at least twice as many pieces as will be used. Careful selection will necessarily result in acceptance of the best pieces. Give these pieces the same considerations given those in the last-mentioned relief, remembering that some may be sanded later for lighter values. Before trying to fit the pieces within the frame, lay them on a large white surface in several possible arrangements, disregarding the final size limitations but considering grain direction, final size and shape. This will help you make decisions about the composition. Cut the pieces as you compose, eventually working the pieces down to the correct sizes for the frame. Spaces between rectangles may vary in

width as long as the variations don't become so great as to attract attention (the narrowest space in the relief shown here is $\frac{9}{16}$″; the widest is $1\frac{1}{16}$″—a variation of $\frac{1}{2}$″, yet not immediately noticeable). Spacing widths between the surrounding frame and the perimeter shapes may also vary, but less so because they tend to be more noticeable. It is more critical that pieces be parallel with the sides of the frame; the eye is very sensitive to non-parallel edges or lines that are supposed to be parallel but aren't. The use of spacer blocks between the frame and perimeter pieces, and between interior pieces, as described in the previous chapter is necessary if the relief is to be laid out precisely.

When you have decided on the composition of the rectangles, cut out each of the concentric circles in the template (located in the center of the heavy-paper section of this book). Any sequence of three or four rings from the seven available ones may be used, from the inside diameter of 3″ to the outside diameter of 10″. You may use four adjacent diameters, or you may alternate some or all of the diameters. Skipping two or more diameters, however, will produce poorly related circles and is apt to be disturbing in an otherwise orderly relief. It is best to try them all, laying four rings over your rectangle composition in many ways before selecting the best circles and positions. Several considerations, both practical and aesthetic, must be made: first, and most important, each circle should involve large enough segments of two, three or four rectangles to be practical to cut; second, the size of the circles should relate to the size of the rectangles; third, the sizes of the segments within the circles should relate; fourth, distances between circles should vary to avoid a static arrangement; and, finally, you should try to avoid a symmetrical arrangement. When you feel you have the best arrangement, lift the whole box onto the floor next to your bench or table, remove any spacing blocks carefully, stand on the top of your bench and take a long look at what you have. The distance you create this way is similar to the usual distance between spectators in a room and the relief.

When you are satisfied with the complete arrangement, tack the template rings to the wood with push-pins and carefully draw around both edges of the rings

**Fig. 11.** The completed relief *Wheels*.

with a soft-lead pencil. To cut them, follow the instructions given in the preceding chapter, except that the inner line of each circle should be cut first, then the outer one. Sand the cut edges when all are cut out.

At this point you must decide which faces are to be sanded and which left as found. Sanding all circle segments but one (as in the model here) is not the only way it may be done. To sand all the circles and none of the remaining rectangles is apt to be too easy and too

pat a solution. The choice must be based on relationships among the pieces, primarily relationships of texture and value.

Mount the pieces as described in the preceding chapter, but with even greater precision. As was mentioned in the beginning of this chapter, if a perfect circle is obviously intended by the artist, then a perfect circle it must be. Using the spacers again will assure you of greater accuracy.

# 4

# Making "Totem"

The word *totem* is of North American Indian origin and refers to animal or plant species believed to be related to a human clan or family. Since the word, in an extended sense, can also mean a symbol of that relationship, artists in the twentieth century have often used the term as a title for works in which simple symbolic shapes of any kind predominate. In the wood relief shown here (Fig. 12), the title derived from the shapes, which are simple and resemble symbols, and from the vertical emphasis of the two columns, which suggest totem poles.

While the work has some similarities to the others we have seen (simple and independent shapes "floated" above a white ground), it is different from them. Here, two vertical forms predominate, surrounded by white space, and both containing (or once containing) all the other parts. It also becomes apparent very quickly that these two pieces were, at one time, one piece, a single board of about four feet in length that made up the whole relief. Next it becomes apparent that the arcs facing each other at the top right relate to the half-circles facing each other at the bottom center, and that all four smaller pieces are derived from the two semicir-cular cutouts of the boards. The horizontal emphasis of both cut pairs tends to tie the two vertical columns together. One then notices that the lighter-colored pieces in each "hole" of the two main columns obvious-ly came from those holes and have been sanded. This becomes even more apparent as you look at the con-tinuation of cracks in each column. In order to achieve variety in the work, some of these pieces were cut in slightly different shapes than the hole. Although the shapes are not true symbols and have no particular meaning, they are few in number and isolated in order to imply that they do have significance. They are also raised slightly above the level of the boards.

Templates are not supplied for this work, so that you will be encouraged to design your own totem. Find an old board with a rugged texture and weathered color. (The one here is oak and came from a pallet.) Bad cracks, knots, nail holes or other defects may help deter-mine the design and cutting pattern. The decision to cut the board in two or to leave it uncut will depend on its length and width. A short, wide board should probably not be cut; a long narrow one probably should be. In either case, the ends of the board (or cut boards) should be honest, that is, any attempt to "rough up" the ends to make them look old, worn or broken is almost always easily detected. Any cuts that must be made should be direct and obviously intended. Cutting a board exactly in half, or exactly in thirds, is apt to produce too precise and static a composition for such an otherwise rough and free-form relief. Think instead of how pieces might be cut from boards to visually extend a shorter length to balance a longer length. The preparation of a full-scale mock-up in brown paper (or cardboard cut with a saber saw) is usually a good idea, even for those with an acute visual imagination. Such a mock-up must take into ac-count the location of features and defects in the actual board(s). Try several designs; as you will find, one will usually lead to another. Shapes should relate without being identical. A unity of texture and value can be achieved in the wood by sanding (or not sanding) some pieces; these elements should be given consideration while planning the piece on paper.

When you have decided on a composition, cut out your patterns, place them on the board(s) and make any final changes or adjustments before drawing around them. Finally, cut the shapes out of the wood, remembering to cut the smaller, inside shapes first in order to hold them more easily. Mount the pieces in the same way as described in the chapter on *Integral*. For variety, the cut-out pieces may protrude above the board surface, as they do here.

**Fig. 12.** The completed relief *Totem*.

# 5

# Making "Symbols"

Many of the shapes in the reliefs discussed so far have suggested familiar objects or seemed similar to natural forms. They have been referred to as symbols, although very few have been particular symbols, recognizable and agreed upon at once by all to have a particular meaning. Often the more abstract a work of art, the more open it is to various interpretations, and the more interesting it is apt to be.

In the wood relief *Symbols* (Fig. 13) there was no attempt either to create specific symbols or to disguise them. As a result, several of the shapes suggest letters of the alphabet (some easy to "read," some requiring an elastic imagination), others may suggest letters of other alphabets or systems of writing (Near and Far Eastern), while still others seem to represent nothing at all but may look like symbols.

This relief differs from the others in several ways: it is a circular form with a black background; the shapes are firmly fixed (rather than floating) and are closely compacted; the shapes are sharp-pointed and composed in a much less organized way. Yet, similarly to the others, the shapes relate in size, value, grain pattern and contrast: the matching parts of several can be found. There is a constant discovery of shapes and their relationships; the negative spaces echo the positive shapes. No area is more important or attracts more attention than another. The work evolved from the area of the author's bench around the power jigsaw. Most of the pieces were scraps from other projects.

To make a relief of random shapes like this one, a power jigsaw is more useful than a saber saw because tighter curves and quicker changes in direction can be made. Begin with scraps that can be collected in the workshop right now (before they are thrown out or burned). Pieces of many thicknesses and every texture wood species and grain pattern can be used. Sand them all down to fresh surface. Those with nail or drill hole add variety. Cut out the pieces, if necessary, without drawing them first and with as little preconceived idea of a pattern as possible.

A circular or elliptical background board relate better to the shapes than a square or rectangle, and the contrast between the perfect order of a circle and the chaos within the circle enhances the work. Size depend only on the number of pieces available to fill the space start with more than enough.

Cut your circle or ellipse carefully from ½" plywood Fill any holes in the core (the layers of plywood) with water putty (see Section IV). When this is completely dry, sand the entire perimeter, slightly beveling the sharp edges. Clean all the dust from the board. Paint the board, including the edge, with two coats of flat black paint.

Begin to arrange your shapes directly on the board from the edge. Glue them down, weight them with small stones or pieces of hardware such as nuts and washers, and clean up oozing glue with a small brush or cotton swabs such as Q-Tips as you go. Work around the perimeter and across the board at the same time Finish the perimeter first, then fill in the remaining area. Vary size, thickness, color and grain pattern as you proceed. Shapes should touch, push, nudge and elbow other shapes; none should be left isolated or touching fewer than two other shapes. When the glue has set, rotate the relief until you find the most satisfactory top-bottom orientation. If you have been completely random in your composition, any orientation will look as good as any other.

Fig. 13. The completed relief *Symbols*.

# Section II

# GEOMETRIC ILLUSIONS IN RELIEF

# 6

# Analysis of an Illusion in Relief: "Upstairs, Downstairs"

Years ago, before there were television-programs-to-eat-breakfast-by, the only thing a kid could do to relieve the boredom of eating his cereal was to read the cereal box. It was on the back of one of those boxes, in a square called "Puzzles and Games," that the author first came across Schröder's Stairs (Fig. 14). Almost everyone has seen this well-known example of perspective reversal and experienced the phenomenon of a geometric figure that changes spontaneously in appearance as one stares at it. The area marked "A" in Schroder's Stairs is seen first as a rear wall, then as a front wall, then again as a rear wall, alternating back and forth. The staircase appears first to be correctly oriented, as it would be climbed. Then, suddenly, the observer is below the stairs looking at the underside. The image continues to be seen alternately one way, then the other, but never both ways at once. In fact, it is difficult to see it simply as a flat, two-dimensional line drawing.

The wood relief *Upstairs, Downstairs* (Fig. 15) is a slight variation of Schröder's Stairs. The ends of the treads and risers meet the front wall and back wall as three 120° angles (or three 60° angles meeting a 180° line) rather than as (in Schröder's) two 135° angles and one 90° angle (or two 45° angles meeting one 270° angle). In both cases, however, the treads/risers are oblique to the observer's line of vision.

Besides these simple angular differences, there is an obvious difference of dimension. The line drawing is just that, a two-dimensional drawing on the page. The relief, however, is both two-dimensional and three-dimensional: nine parallelograms of ½"-thick boards, all in the same plane, and mounted on a piece of plywood cut to accommodate them. A space is created between the parallelograms which becomes the "line." The figure is dependent on this "line" for its illusion, and the illusion is heightened by the difference in color (brown and gray in the actual relief, seen as value in the black-and-white photograph) between the treads/risers and the walls. The artist's intention is to further confuse an already puzzling figure by introducing a *real* third dimension into an *illusion* of three dimensions.

The elements of design considered important to the free-form reliefs in the preceding section are just as important to geometric illusions. Relationships of texture, value, color and grain pattern, and the effects of light, are very important in creating the illusion of an object having horizontal planes (tops) and vertical planes (sides). Careful selection of the boards to be used is even more important in illusions because each of these relationships will affect the success of the relief.

In *Upstairs, Downstairs*, for instance, each of the pieces used for treads/risers had to be identical for the illusion of perspective reversal to work well. Cutting all of them from the same board was the only way to achieve this, so the length of the board determined the number and length of the treads/risers. Sanding some pieces for lighter values and texture variations is sometimes desirable or necessary (sanding pieces from several different boards will not necessarily produce uniform color or value, however). Grain patterns in an illusion can also help differentiate planes, but "wild" or very pronounced patterns (such as that of Douglas fir) will distract from and interfere with the illusion, lessening the impact. The most desirable woods to use are

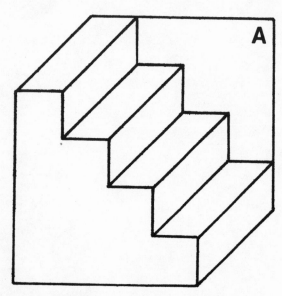

**Fig. 14.** Schröder's Stairs.

[Text resumes after template section.]

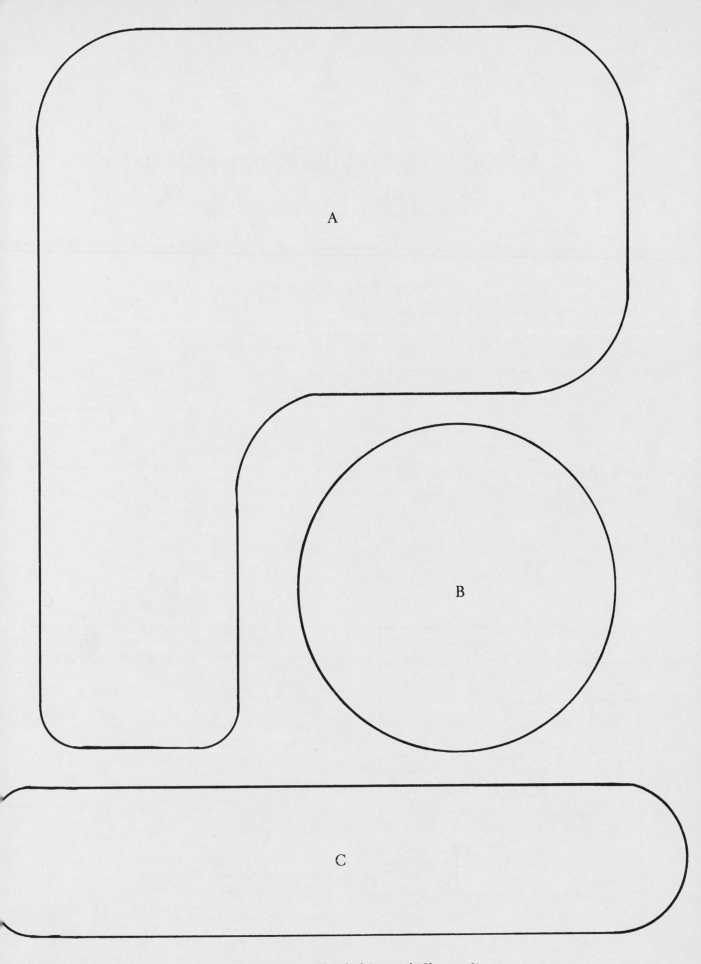

Templates for the Wood Relief *Integral* (Chapter 2)
(See Fig. 10 for position of lettered pieces)

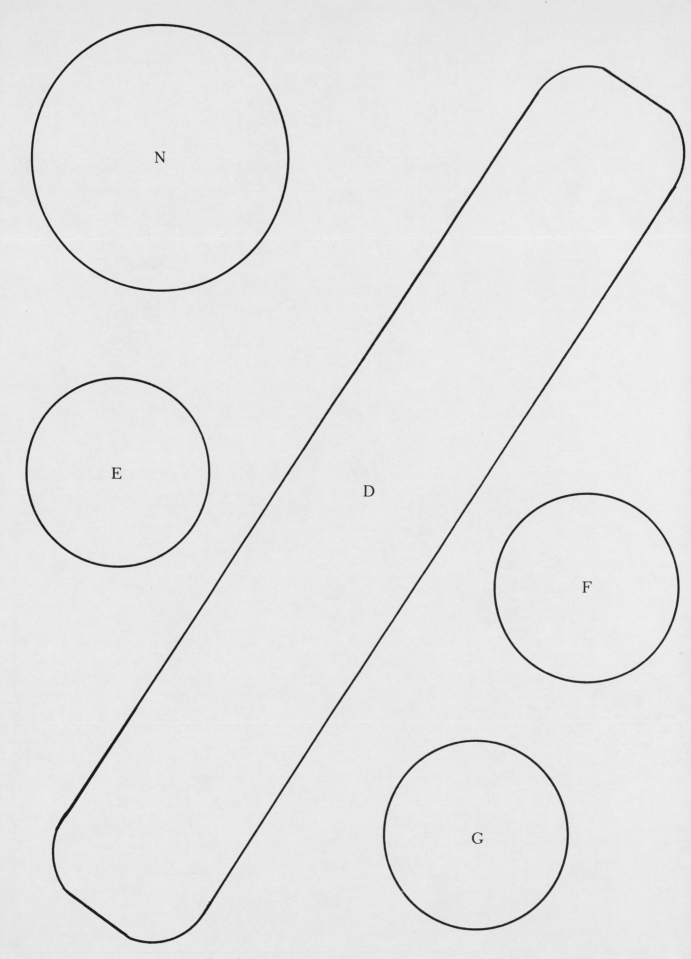

Templates for the Wood Relief *Integral* (Chapter 2)
(See Fig. 10 for position of lettered pieces)

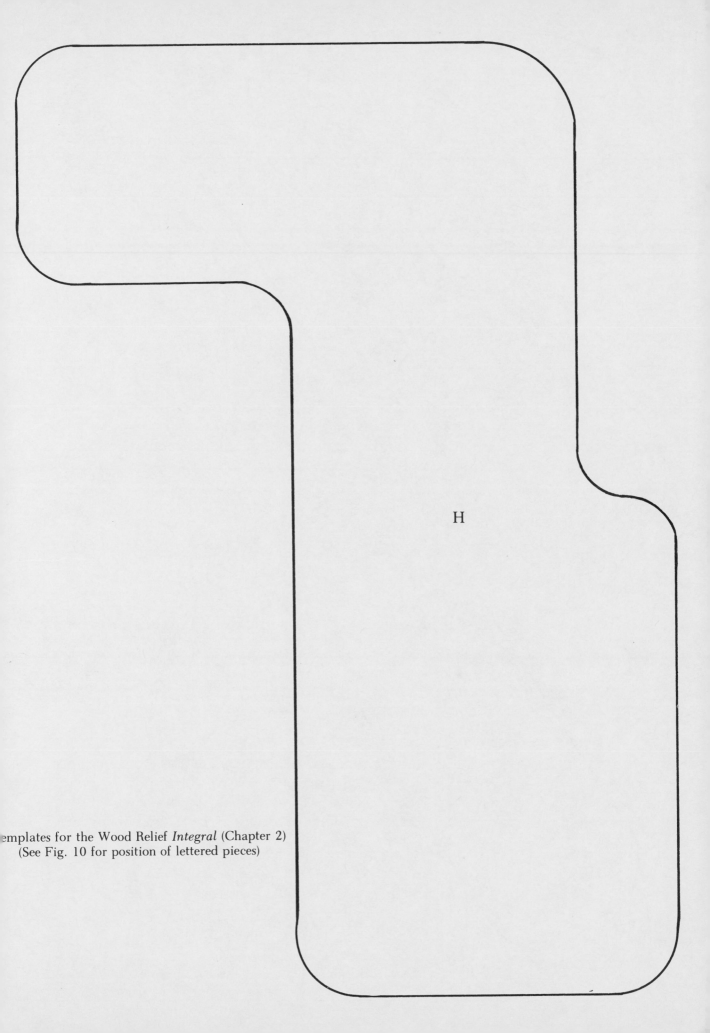

H

Templates for the Wood Relief *Integral* (Chapter 2)
(See Fig. 10 for position of lettered pieces)

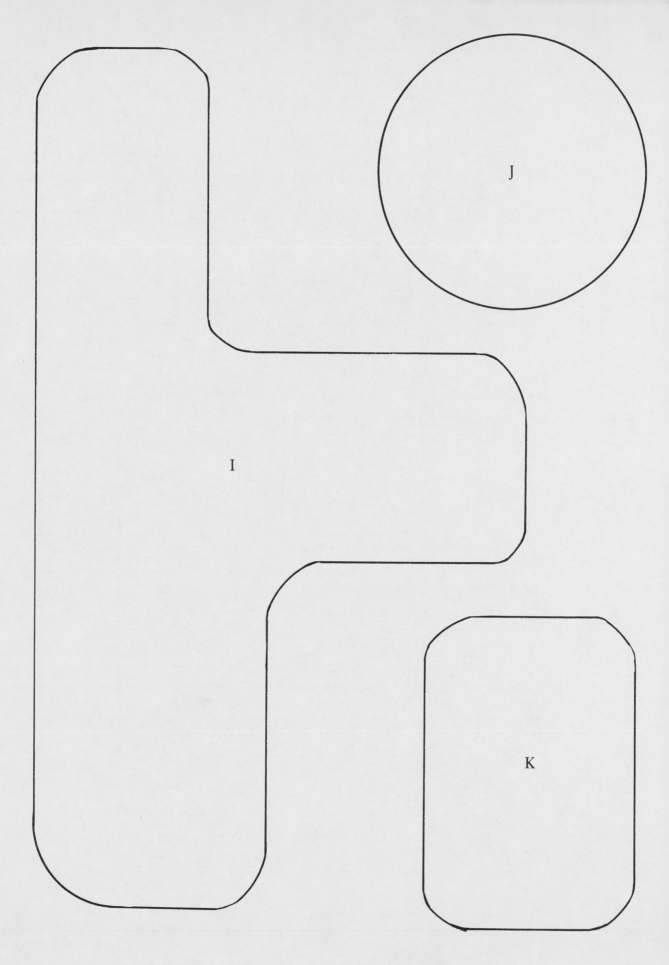

Templates for the Wood Relief *Integral* (Chapter 2)
(See Fig. 10 for position of lettered pieces)

Templates for the Wood Relief *Integral* (Chapter 2)
(See Fig. 10 for position of lettered pieces)

Templates for the Wood Relief *Wheels* (Chapter 3)

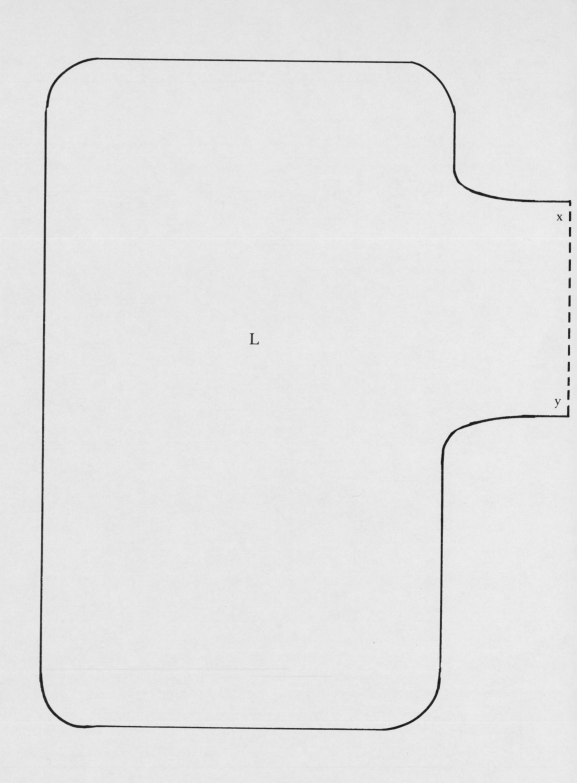

L

x

y

Templates for the Wood Relief *Integral* (Chapter 2)
(See Fig. 10 for position of lettered pieces)

Templates for the Wood Relief *Integral* (Chapter 2)
(See Fig. 10 for position of lettered pieces)

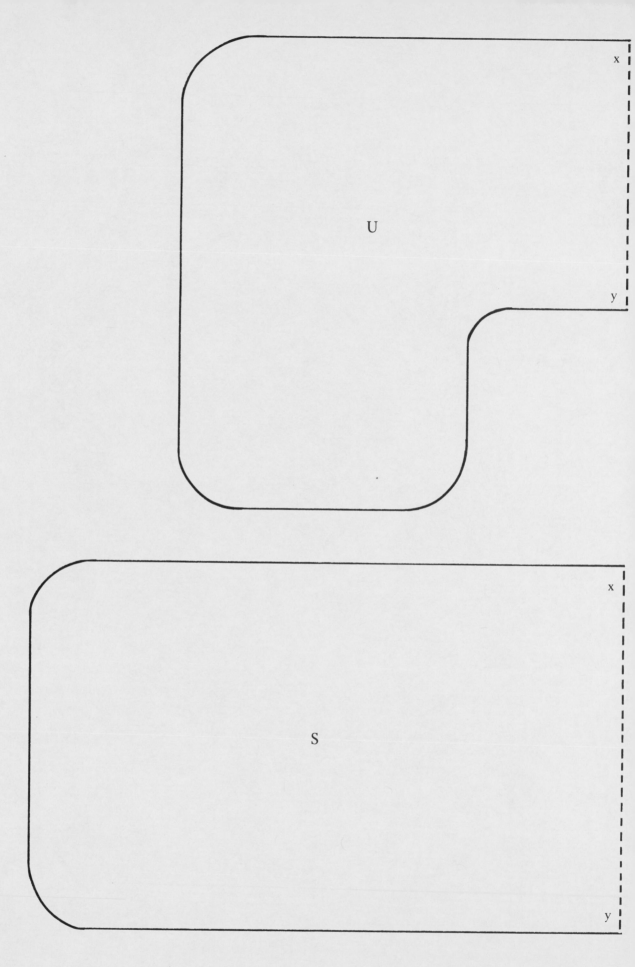

Templates for the Wood Relief *Integral* (Chapter 2)
(See Fig. 10 for position of lettered pieces)

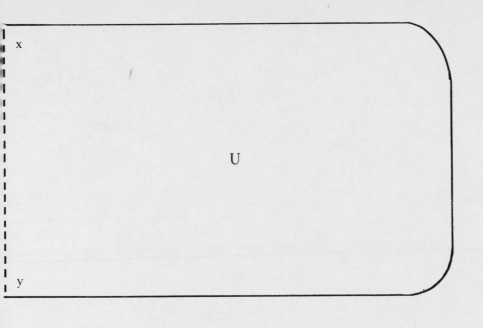

x

U

y

x

S

y

Templates for the Wood Relief *Integral* (Chapter 2)
(See Fig. 10 for position of lettered pieces)

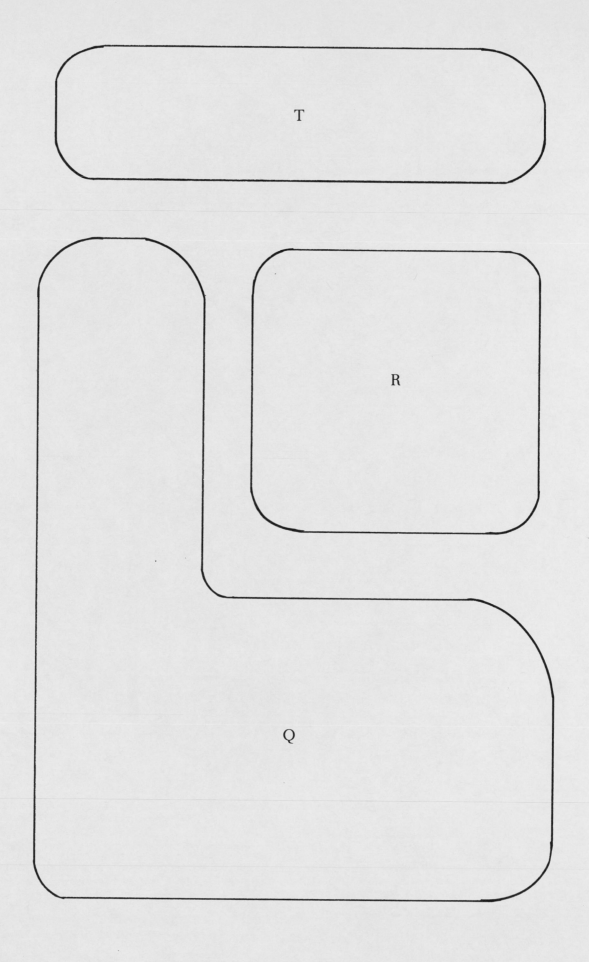

Templates for the Wood Relief *Integral* (Chapter 2)
(See Fig. 10 for position of lettered pieces)

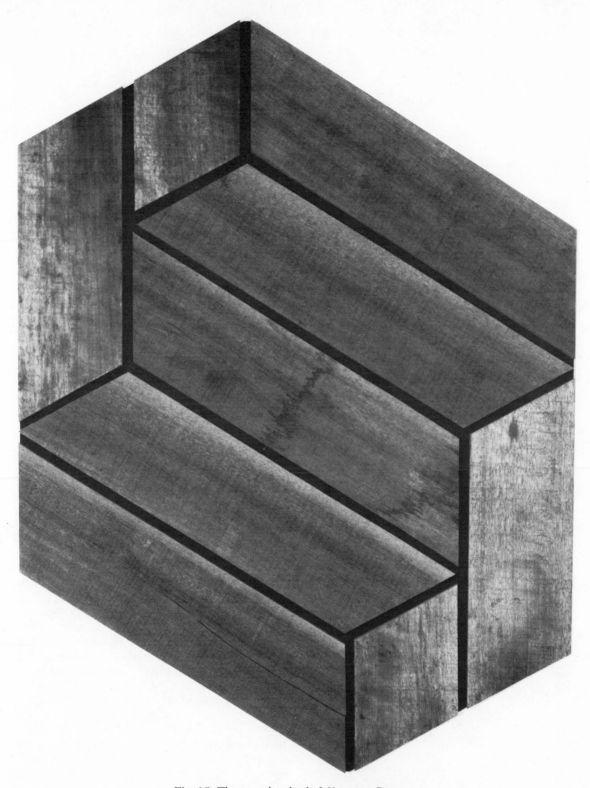

**Fig. 15.** The completed relief *Upstairs, Downstairs*.

those with fine or small-patterned grains. Basswood, beech, birch, boxwood, buckeye, holly, most mahoganies, poplar, sycamore and black walnut are some of the finer-grained species. Certainly there are others, and you should not restrict yourself to purchased lumber. All of the reliefs in this section were made of found lumber, most of which is Philippine mahogany.

# 7

# Making "Upstairs, Downstairs"

The tools you will need for making these illusions in relief are: a crosscut saw, a table saw (with sharp blade, miter gauge and fence), a good folding ruler, two large plastic drafting triangles (one 45°, one 30°/60°), a bevel gauge, a ¼" power drill (with a ³⁄₁₆" bit and a countersink bit), several C-clamps, a screwdriver and several spacers ⁷⁄₁₆" thick. Materials needed are: a selected board at least 4½" wide by ⅝"–¾" thick and 8' long; another board of the same width and thickness and at least 40" long, but contrasting in color or value; a piece of ½" plywood 24" x 30", a dozen and a half 1"-x-#10 flat-head wood screws, 24" of 50-lb.-test picture wire and two ¾"-x-#10 round-head wood screws.

Since these illusions are made up almost entirely of miter-cut boards, it is essential that your miter cutting be accurate. To assist in accuracy, screw an extension board to the face of your miter gauge and face *it* smoothly with #80 grit sandpaper (Fig. 16). This will help to keep your work from creeping into or away from the blade while you are pushing it through. Still, the piece is apt to pivot on the corner of the miter gauge unless it is held very tightly against the face while cutting. Hold-down clamps, available to fit some miter gauges, are helpful if the piece being cut is no longer

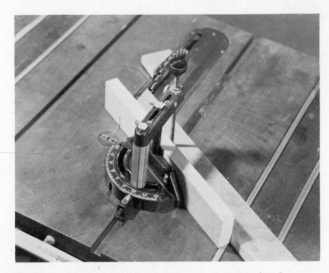

**Fig. 16.** Miter gauge, with extension, set at 30° right of center.

than any in these reliefs. Be sure to use a clamp pad to avoid marring the surface of your boards.

Begin by ripping about ¹⁄₁₆" from both edges of both boards to a finished width of 4⅜". Cut the 8' board into five pieces, each 18½" long. This length allows more than enough for two thicknesses of the saw teeth (the kerf). Using the 30°/60° triangle, mark a line at one corner 60° from the edge on three of the five board pieces. Set your miter gauge at 30° to the right of center and cut the three boards (cut all the pieces for this relief using the gauge slot to the right of the blade). Mark the other two boards of the five in the same way but from the opposite edge of the boards. Set your miter gauge at 30° to the *left* of center and cut these two boards. From the points you have produced on all the boards, measure along each edge 15½" and mark another line with the triangle parallel to the first cut. Set your gauge at 30° to the right of center again, cut three boards, reset it at 30° to the left of center and cut the other two. The "steps" of the relief are now ready to mount.

To make the "walls," cut the 40" board in half. Again, on each half, mark a line at one corner 60° from the edge. Set the gauge at 30° to the right of center and cut both. From each point, measure 5¼" and cut both boards, making sure that your line is on the *left* side of the saw blade to produce a full 5¼" piece. Along the edges of the remaining pieces, measure 11" from the points, make lines parallel to the ends just cut, and cut them, this time making sure that the lines are on the *right* side of the saw blade to produce full 11" pieces. You now have the nine pieces needed for the relief.

To make the plywood base, lay out the pieces on the face as they will be positioned, using the ⁷⁄₁₆" spacers. Since there are no 90° corners in the base, the layout must be done with care, using one finished (or "factory") edge of the plywood as a starting edge. Look at the relief when all pieces are positioned to make sure that points are opposite each other, that edges are parallel, and that each piece is in the best position in relation to the others. Holding each firmly in position, draw around the outside pieces to produce the perimeter line. Remove all the pieces from the base, keeping each in its relative position to the others. Check your perimeter lines with the drafting triangle and a square.

When you are sure of the lines, cut them with either a bandsaw or the table saw.

Sand all edges of the shaped base, fill holes in the core with water-soluble putty, sand again when dry, and replace the pieces in their proper positions. While holding each, trace around it lightly with a pencil to produce an accurate line drawing of the relief on the base. Paint the spaces of this line drawing and the entire perimeter. These areas should be wider than necessary to assure that no "white spots" will be seen when the relief is assembled. When the paint is dry, mark two screw-hole locations on each of the nine sections of the base, positioning them in opposite corners about 1½" from the edge of each section. Drill a ³⁄₁₆" hole through the base at each mark. Turn the base over and drill countersink depressions in each hole.

To mount the pieces, clamp the base, face up, to your bench, allowing it to overhang the edge about one third. Clamp at least three adjacent pieces to the base in their proper positions (using spacers between them, and clamp pads to avoid marring them). Working from below, drill a shallow pilot hole into the clamped pieces through the countersunk holes. Drive flat-head screws as each hole is drilled. Remove the clamps when both screws are in a piece, and clamp another adjacent piece in its correct position.

To hang the relief, drive ¾" round-head screws part way into the back about 1" in from the edges and 4"–5" above a center "equator" line (making sure the screw will not enter a space on the front). Stretch the heavy-duty picture wire taut between the screws and twist it tightly. Drive the screws in as far as they will go. Your relief is ready to hang.

# 8

# Making "Stable"

This relief (Fig. 17), with a title suggestive of horse stalls, is also a perspective-reversal figure but is not quite as perfect as Schröder's Stairs. In the latter (and in *Upstairs, Downstairs*) every piece functions logically, either as tread or riser or back wall or front wall, no matter which way the stairs appear to be directed. In *Stable*, however, the top three (light-colored) pieces and the corresponding bottom three pieces cannot be reconciled as having a logical architectural position. The three "stalls" may appear to have "floors" between the dark dividing "partitions," but as your eye wanders to the top of the partitions, the direction of entry to the stalls suddenly changes and the three now have "ceilings" but no floors, something like suspended dividers between pay telephones. What was the "floor" now becomes part of the "back wall," or, as seen originally, what was the "ceiling" now becomes "back wall." But in either case it is an *uneasy* back wall, not really part of the unchanging back wall—the three rectangular pieces between the dark partitions. Trying to fix the "ceiling" or "floor" pieces in space only results in reversing the perspective again.

Part of the reason for the success of this illusion is the height of the stalls. If the back walls and partitions were shorter, the eye could focus on both the "floor" and "ceiling" pieces at once, and the perspective would not reverse as well.

To make *Stable* you will need the same tools listed for *Upstairs, Downstairs*. Materials needed are: a selected board, dark in value, 4" wide by ⅝"–¾" thick by 72" long; another board, light in value, of the same width and thickness but at least 74" long; 26 flat-head screws 1" x #10; 50-lb.-test picture wire at least 32" long; two

¾"-x-#10 round-head wood screws: and a piece of plywood ½" x 24" x 30".

Begin by ripping both boards to 3¾" wide. If the boards are longer than the minimum lengths given above, select the best sections for use in the relief. With a 45° triangle, mark a line at one corner 45° from the edge of the dark board (Fig. 18). Set your miter gauge at 45° to the right of center, clamp the board to the gauge and slowly make the cut. With the gauge at 45° there is a greater chance of the board slipping or pivoting while going through the saw. Take whatever time is necessary to clamp the board securely to the gauge in order to prevent this. When the first cut is made, measure along the edge 16½" from the point and mark another 45° line parallel to the cut. As you clamp this piece in preparation for cutting, remember that the marked line must be on the left side of the saw blade to produce a full 16½" piece. Mark, clamp and cut the next two pieces in the same way. The fourth (last) piece will have to be marked and turned around before cutting, of course, in order to clamp it to the gauge.

In the light-colored board, it is best to make the 90° cuts first. Cut three pieces 11⅞" long. Next, move your miter gauge to the slot on the left side of the blade, and set the gauge at 45° to the left of center. Mark the first cut 7¾" from the bottom edge of the board and make the cut. Measure 7¾" from the point produced and mark a 90° angle across the board. Reset the gauge to 90° and make the cut. Measure and alternate angle (45°, 90°) for each cut on the remaining board to produce the six top and bottom pieces of the relief.

The plywood base is made, and the pieces mounted in the same manner as for *Upstairs, Downstairs*.

**Fig. 17.** The completed relief *Stable*.

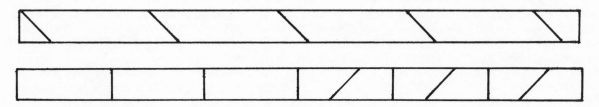

**Fig. 18.** Boards marked for cutting *Stable*.

# 9

# Making "Corner Cube"

The first two illusions that have been presented are examples of simple perspective reversal, in which planes seem to turn "in" or "out" spontaneously while one is looking at the figure. In its simplest form, perspective reversal takes place when looking at a perspective drawing of a cube, which will alternately appear to be a solid form one moment and a space defined by walls a moment later. The illusion of three dimensions in either configuration is increased by varying the value tones of the three parallelograms: a light top, one dark side which appears to be in deep shadow, and one moderately dark side (a middle value) which appears to get some light. The illusion that this is a solid form is most apparent because of this shading, but it is not difficult to voluntarily (or involuntarily) reverse this illusion to see a space defined by walls.

In *Corner Cube* (Fig. 19) two simple cubes are presented, one of which is smaller, shaded in a reverse pattern to the other and turned upside down. (The shaded portions of this photograph are brown and grey in the original.) Because two figures are involved, they each go in and out. It would seem, then, that four ways of seeing the whole figure would be possible: both cubes in, both out, the larger cube out while the smaller is in, and the smaller cube out while the larger is in. Actually the relief can be seen best in only three ways: as a small cube projecting toward us and hiding the point of a large cube; as a large cube with its nearest corner—one eighth of it—cut out; and as the upper corner of a room with a cube (such as a hi-fi speaker) hung in it. (Some observers have tilted their heads slightly and have made out the bottom corner of a tiled shower with a built-in bench).

For this large relief you will need the same tools as for the last two reliefs. A dado set for your table saw is very helpful but is not absolutely necessary. For materials you will need: three carefully selected boards of light, dark and middle values, each 3″ wide (finished) by ⅝″–¾″ thick by 12′ long. (Wider but shorter boards may be ripped into 3″-wide pieces, of course; you will need six 24″ pieces of each.) The ½″ plywood base should be at least 39″ x 45″. You will also need 63 flat-head screws 1″ x #10, 50-lb.-test picture wire at least 42″ long, and two round-head wood screws 1″ x #10.

The perfect alignment of what appear to be 108 separate pieces is achieved by dadoing only 27 pieces, nine of which are less than 24″ long and 18 of which are less than 13″ long.

For cutting all the pieces, the miter gauge should be set at 30° to the right of center and used in the slot to the right of the saw blade. Begin by cutting three lengths of each board 22⅞₆″, measured from angle to angle along the edge. Next, cut six lengths of each board 11¼₆″, measured the same way. You now have nine long pieces and 18 short pieces.

Replace your saw blade with dado blades set to cut a dado ¼″ wide by ⅜″ deep. Reset the miter gauge at 30° to the left of center and move it to the slot left of the blade. The fence should be set to the right of the blade 3″ from the right edge of the teeth. (Without a dado set, repeated passes over the regular blade must be made; the fence must be repositioned at least twice to make ¼″ rabbets or slots 3″ apart.) Dado one end of all 27 pieces to produce a 3″-x-3″ diamond parallelogram at the end of each board. Turn them around and dado the other end of each board. The 18 short pieces are now ready to mount. Reset the fence 6¼″ from the blade and dado each end of the nine long pieces. Finally, reset the fence 9½″ from the blade and cut the final dado in the nine long pieces.

It is easier to paint the dadoes you have just made before they are mounted on the base than after. Use a fine camel's-hair brush and the same paint that is used for the base.

In laying out the pieces to cut and paint the base, begin with one long piece clamped to a finished edge of the plywood and a straightedge clamped at 120° to that finished edge. Use ¼″ spacers between every two pieces as they are laid out. Following Figure 19, lay out all 27 pieces (noting the grain direction) and proceed to complete the relief according to the directions given for *Upstairs, Downstairs.* Use three screws for each of the long pieces and two screws for each of the short pieces.

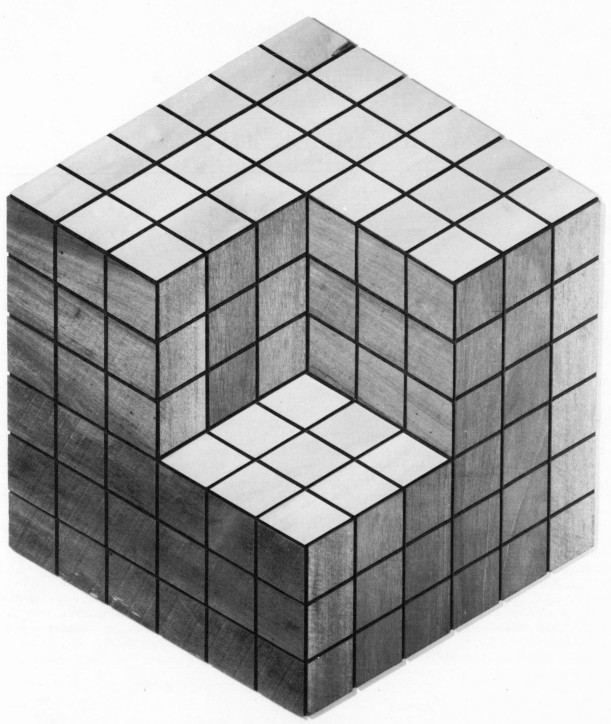

**Fig. 19.** The completed relief *Corner Cube*.

# 10

# Making "Hole in Nine"

It is obvious upon looking at *Hole in Nine* (Fig. 20) that there is no perspective-reversal phenomenon taking place. This relief is a simple depth illusion of nine square and identical boxes or tunnels that open directly into real space. Both illusion and reality are combined to pose the age-old question of what is real. In addition to this idea, however, there are other interesting illusions which appear as one looks at the relief longer. Most apparent, perhaps, is the image of four crosses with beveled arms joined together. There is also a strong awareness of the lines that separate the individual pieces. Although it may not be immediately apparent, it is necessary to the illusion that the right and bottom pieces of each square should be of a lighter value than the left and top pieces.

One square alone would not have been satisfactory; the relief would have looked like a picture frame. Four squares are better, and nine squares are better still. Sixteen or 25 squares tend to become overall patterns, not necessarily without interest, but losing some of their individuality.

Tools needed are the same as for the other illusionistic reliefs, with the addition of a saber saw. Materials needed are: two boards of similar texture but of dark and light values respectively, each 2½" wide (finished) by 10' (as with *Corner Cube*, a wider board may be ripped into 2½" widths). Also needed are a ½" plywood base 27½" square, six dozen flat-head wood screws 1" x #10, 50-lb.-test picture wire 33" long, and two round-head wood screws 1" x #10.

Begin by setting the miter gauge at 45° to the right of center and using the saw-table slot to the right of the blade. From each board cut nine pieces 12½" long, measured from angle to angle along the edge. Now set the miter gauge at 45° to the left of center and use the slot to the left of the blade. From the point at each end of each piece, measure 8⅝" and, using a 45° triangle, mark two parallel lines across each piece. Cut each piece in half between these lines. Although this should not really be necessary, any excess should be trimmed or sanded from any of the 36 pieces that are not 8⅝" long. When mounted, each square will measure 9" x 9" with a 4"-x-4" hole.

Nine holes must be cut in the base. Be sure the base is a perfect square 27½" x 27½". Across the top and bottom, measure and mark the following dimensions in sequence: 2½", 4", 5¼", 4", 5¼", 4", 2½". Lightly connect the marks, turn the base one quarter-turn, then measure and mark the dimensions again. Connect only the 4" distances with a line dark enough to see and darken the first 4" lines drawn. Cut out each square carefully with a saber saw and finish all edges with sandpaper and water putty. After painting all edges and exposed face lines, bore two screw holes for each piece. Clamp one row of "boxes" in position across the base (using ¼" spacers) before screwing any pieces in place. Use a square and straightedge frequently to assure perfect 90° corners and aligned edges. When all pieces are finally screwed in position, stretch the hanging wire tightly across the back between the top horizontal row of boxes and the center horizontal row.

**Fig. 20.** The completed relief *Hole in Nine*.

# Section III

# WOODEN PUZZLES
# IN RELIEF

# 11

# Analysis of a Puzzle in Relief: "How Many Squares Can You Count?"

This relief (Fig. 21) was suggested by a magazine advertisement in which the same question was asked beneath a square of several different colors divided into similar segments with black lines. The colors related to each other and to the square in no discernible way but were apparently used to attract attention to the ad. They did not seem to make the challenge of counting squares either harder or easier.

Although this relief and the others in this section are similar in technique to both free-form reliefs and geometric illusions, their form and intent are different. *How Many Squares?* is neither made up of symbols and suggestive shapes, nor is it an illusion of depth and perspective. It is a pattern puzzle to be solved by the observer if he wishes to take the time. It may be similar in idea (though not in fact) to the infinite linear patterns found in Islamic designs, or to the frets and band designs found in ancient Greek architecture. Neither of these traditions served as a direct source of these puzzles for the author, however.

The challenge offered in the title is one of perception, in which the observer must look beyond the overall pattern to parts superimposed on each other. The solid squares are simple enough to count, beginning with the smallest. The four smallest ones centered in the top half of the relief plus the four centered in the bottom half add up to eight, and each of these groups makes up another square four times its size (giving 10 so far). The four horizontal rows of four squares each, add another 16 (making 26). If each of the first three squares in the top three rows is seen as the top left quarter of a larger square, another nine squares can be added (making 35). When you count in the squares created by nine of these basic 16, four more squares are added (making 39). Finally, all the pieces within the frame make up one square, for a total of 40.

The elements of design that were important to the free-form reliefs in the first section continue to be im-portant to these reliefs. In *How Many Squares?* the relationship of shapes is essential: all pieces are made up of perfect squares and symmetrical L-shaped corners. The element of size is determined partly by the material available and partly by the complexity of the design. A large relief is usually more effective than a small one (the original of this one is 43″ square). Whereas contrast of texture, value and grain pattern were desirable in the free-form and illusionistic reliefs, the sameness of all these elements is desirable here. Preferably all the pieces should come from the same board or from the same structure. The appeal of the relief must come from its principal intention—the creation of a simple puzzle to be solved—rather than from a contrast of its parts. A variety of woods, colors, grains, etc. can (as in the illusions) interfere with this intent. Contrast *is* found between the roughness of the weathered boards and the sharp-cut angles of the precise squares. It is also found between the color and texture of the weathered wood and the color and texture of the fresh saw cuts. Further, a dynamic quality is created in the brighter light seen at the intersection of the vertical and horizontal spaces. This is the result of light reaching the intersection from two directions. The effect changes with the varying light of day and when the relief is hung is different locations.

The "lines" created by the spaces between the pieces in these reliefs are of even greater importance than those in either free-form reliefs or geometric illusions. In the earlier reliefs, the shapes and color values of the pieces determined the pattern, i.e., line was of secondary importance to shape. In the puzzle reliefs, the lines determine the pattern.

These puzzles are an extension and variation of the relief *Wheels*, presented earlier in this book: they are patterns superimposed on other patterns. This observation should give the reader ideas for future reliefs. The possibilities are endless.

**Fig. 21.** The completed relief *How Many Squares Can You Count?*

# 12

# Making "How Many Squares?"

The size of this relief will depend on the width of the board you select to use. It should be as wide as possible, but must also be 16 times longer than its width, plus a couple of inches to allow for 15 saw kerfs. Since you must cut sixteen *squares*, the width will determine their length. For example, a board 6″ wide must be 8′, plus 2″, long; a board 8″ wide must be 10′ 8″, plus 2″, long. A board narrower than 6″ would be best used in another relief; it will be too narrow to have much impact in this one. Two boards may be used effectively if they are close to being identical in color, grain pattern, texture and value. Boards with a strong grain pattern, rich coloring or a weathered texture are most desirable.

Begin by checking the edges of the board to determine that it is not so marred or scarred that it needs to be ripped to a narrower width. When the width is determined, and a fresh starting end is cut, lay out the first basic square, measuring it to the same length as the width. Disregard knots and other defects; full cracks that separate or loose knots that fall out can usually be glued together again. Alternately mark and cut 16 basic squares, laying each in order on a clean surface as you progress. Squares may be cut by hand, with a radial-arm saw, a table saw or a portable circular saw. If using the latter, turn the board good side down; if using a table saw, first cut the board into manageable lengths by hand, allowing enough length on each piece for saw kerfs.

When all 16 squares are cut, lay out rows of four on a light-surfaced table, spacing them at identical intervals by means of spacer blocks. The proper space must be determined by trial and error, but as a general rule larger squares require wider spacing (e.g., up to an inch). The spaces in the actual relief shown in the photo are ¾″ for squares that measure 9¼″ x 9¼″. Pieces in each row of squares should be kept in the order of cutting, but whole rows may be arranged at will for better distribution of grain pattern, knot location, color, etc.

When the proper spacing and layout of the basic squares are determined, the eight small squares in the center of the top and bottom halves must be marked for cutting. The size of each of these small squares is one half the size of the basic squares, less one half the width of the spaces. For the relief shown here this was determined by dividing the basic square width in half (giving 4⅝″) and then subtracting half the width of the space (⅜″). Thus, these small squares are 4¼″ x 4¼″. Together with the ¾″ space between them they measure 9¼″, the same size as the basic squares.

Following the photograph, mark each square in the proper corner for cutting, and at the same time mark the cutting line for the space surrounding each of these small squares. The width of this space should be the same as all other spaces. The small square itself should be cut first, on the waste side of the marked line. This may be done with any of the saws mentioned above, but care must be taken not to cut into the L-shape of the basic square. If a circular saw of any kind is used, the full cut cannot be made; the cut must be finished with a hand saw, then sanded to account for the different widths of the saw blades.

When all the pieces are cut, the box frame should be made as described in Section IV. The inside size of this frame is determined by adding up the measurements of the four basic squares and the five spaces. Dowel posts, of ⅜″ to ½″ diameter, should then be set in the pieces and mounted in the box frame, as described in Section I, Chapter 2. Spacer blocks must be used throughout the process to keep the pieces accurately aligned.

# 13

# Making "81 Squares"

This relief (Fig. 22) is another puzzle challenging the ability of the observer to see superimposed figures. Although there are only 49 pieces within the frame, there are 81 squares to be counted. A unit measure of 3" (the smallest pieces) may be used for counting: there are eight 3" squares, 25 6" (the basic squares), eight 9", 17 12", four 15", nine 18", four 21", five 24", one 27" and one 30".

The 25 basic squares may be taken from a single board, or they may be taken from boards that have weathered or worn together. Those pictured here came from a discarded pallet, and were kept in the order in which they were nailed down. (Since most pallets are made in the same mill that cut the logs, these boards probably came from the same tree.) Basic squares of from 5" to 7" are best; they will make a relief with an outside frame width and height of from 31" to 41". For these instructions it will be assumed they are 6" squares, spaced ¾" apart, and cut with a table saw. Again, any saw may be used providing the cuts are kept accurate and allowance is made for the kerf widths.

When the boards have been selected and the width determined, cut the 25 basic squares, keeping them in order throughout the construction.

Next, set the fence 3" to the right of the blade and, using the numbered diagram (Fig. 23), cut the following squares fully through, being careful to orient them correctly before pushing them into the blade. Cut numbers 2, 3, 4, 6, 8, 10, 11, 12, 14, 15, 16, 18, 20, 22, 23 and 24, returning both halves of each square to their respective positions in the layout. For cutting the corner squares, clamp a stop-stick to the fence to prevent the square from being pushed too far into the saw. Without moving the fence, make one of the cuts in the squares numbered 1, 5, 7, 9, 17, 19, 21 and 25. Next, move the fence to the left of the blade and 3" from the left side of the teeth. Clamp the stop to the right side of the fence. Make the second cut in each of the squares just numbered, and return it to its position in the layout. When this step is completed, finish cutting out the corners of each square with a hand saw, returning both pieces to the layout.

Next, the proper space (the "line") must be cut within each basic square. This width may be between one half and two thirds the width of the spaces between the basic squares. Here it is two thirds the width, i.e., ½". Reset the fence 2½" to the right of the blade. Each of the *smaller* pieces (those closer to the center of the relief) of all 25 squares may now be cut to a 2½" width. Be sure it is the *inside* edge of each piece that gets cut. Return each to its correct position in the layout. Two posts (¼"–½" in diameter) must be mounted in each piece in the relief except the eight smallest squares, for which one post will suffice. Make a box frame as described in Section IV, and mount the pieces carefully, using spacer blocks for perfect alignment.

Fig. 22. The completed relief *81 Squares*.

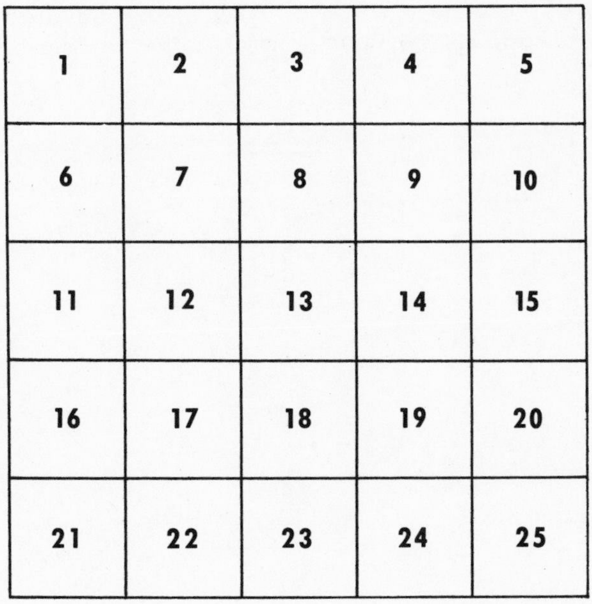

| 1 | 2 | 3 | 4 | 5 |
|---|---|---|---|---|
| 6 | 7 | 8 | 9 | 10 |
| 11 | 12 | 13 | 14 | 15 |
| 16 | 17 | 18 | 19 | 20 |
| 21 | 22 | 23 | 24 | 25 |

Fig. 23. Working diagram for *81 Squares*.

# 14

# Making "Nine and Nine"

The ways of seeing this wood relief (Fig. 24) are numerous. As the title implies, it is first perceived as a symmetrical pattern of nine large squares enclosing nine smaller squares. Soon, however, it can be seen as 36 squares (six rows of six), each with a square corner cut out that makes up one quarter of another square. Further observation begins to reveal many more squares and other patterns such as crosses and brackets. Longer study will reveal no less than 136 squares to be counted: 36 2½" squares (the smallest pieces), 45 5" (including the 36 basic squares), 25 10", 16 15", nine 20", four 25" and one 30". Finally, the questions of perception arise (as they do with all the reliefs in Sections II and III): how are we able to isolate patterns within patterns, and voluntarily change what we see at will?

As with the other two reliefs in this section, a board (or boards) of uniform texture and color (and adequate length) should be selected. (The relief in the photo was made of a single board 5" wide by 15'6" long.) When the board width and space width are determined, the board should be cut into 36 squares.

In this relief the smallest squares have been cut to the same width as each leg of the larger basic squares. Both are 2¼" wide. If a 5" square with ½" spaces is used, set the saw fence at 2¼" to the right of the blade. A 6" square with ½" spaces will require a fence setting of 2¾". In each case one half of the space width is subtracted from one half of the square width to get the fence setting. Clamp a stop-stick to the fence to avoid cutting too deep. Saw into each of the 36 pieces. Once again, it is important that all pieces be kept in a correct layout order as you progress.

When all pieces have been cut, move the fence 2¼" to the left of the blade, reclamp the stop-stick, and make the second cut in all the pieces. Finish cutting out the corners of all the squares with a hand saw. Finally, trim all 36 of the smallest squares to 2¼".

The inside dimensions of the box frame will be six times the width of the squares plus seven times the width of the spaces; this one measures 33½" (6 x 5" plus 7 x ½").

One hundred eight posts (¼"–⅜" in diameter) must be cut and mounted in the 72 pieces of this relief (two posts in each L-shaped piece and one in each small square). When all the posts are firmly glued in the pieces, mount each in the box frame, using spacer blocks.

**Fig. 24.** The completed relief *Nine and Nine*.

# Section IV

# FRAMING AND FINISHING

# Framing and Finishing

For all but one of the reliefs in Sections I and III, a box frame must be made. In each case the size of the relief will determine the size of the frame. Because of this the frame must be made after the pieces of the relief have been cut and laid out.

The backing board on which all the pieces are mounted is a sheet of ½" plywood of "A-C" grade. This should be cut to the dimensions of the relief *plus* the surrounding space. This space should be the same width as, or, sometimes, slightly wider than, the space between the pieces. No matter what saw is used for cutting the plywood, edges must be straight and corners must be square.

A miter joint, which will be described, is the best kind of corner, although butt joints may be used. The framing walls are made of 1"-x-3" clear white pine. To determine the length needed, add up the four edges of the cut plywood back, then add eight inches, or two inches per side. For the larger reliefs in Section III, this may give a total length too long to be easily managed. Two pieces, each half the length, may be easier to handle. From this stock cut the four framing walls, each at least two inches longer than the edge it will be on. Using a combination square or other 45° angle, mark the angle on the edge, at one end, of each of the framing walls. Tilt the arbor of your table saw exactly 45° and, using the miter gauge to hold each piece, cut off the 45° end you have just marked.

At this point it is wise to number each edge of the plywood back and, correspondingly, each framing wall. Choose the best edges of the walls for the front edges of the frame. Next, measure each edge of the plywood carefully and mark the same measurement at 45° on the corresponding wall, measuring from the shortest side of the cut end. Measure and cut each of the walls.

The plywood back should now be laid flat on a large table or bench with each framing wall in its correct position for joining to the back. All four corners should come together perfectly and enclose the back snugly. Any piece that is too long may be shaved down to the proper length, but pieces that are too short must be cut again.

When all walls fit perfectly, each should be laid flat with the outer side up and three 6d finish nails started in the wood. Drive two nails about 4" from each end and ¼" in from the back edge. Drive the third nail halfway between these two, and also ¼" in from the back edge. All three nails should be driven into the wood until the point protrudes slightly.

A liberal coat of glue should be spread along one edge of the back, and the first framing wall nailed in place. Glue and nail each wall in place around the perimeter, also gluing each mitered corner as you proceed. When the four walls are glued and nailed, the nails must be driven below the surface with a nail set. Before the glue dries, stand the finished frame on edge on a clean floor and drive two 6d nails through each mitered corner—one from each end of each wall. This should be done with care, keeping each corner perfectly square. The nails should be set.

When the nailing is completed and the glue is dry, all holes in the frame and back should be filled with a wood putty. A water-soluble putty made of powder is easiest to use, very effective and not expensive. After adequate drying time, the entire frame should be lightly sanded with a fine sandpaper (#150 or finer) wrapped around a wood block. All corners and edges should be slightly rounded or beveled to avoid chipping out or splintering.

When the sanding is completed, the frame is ready to paint. Wipe all dust from the frame with a rag and apply two coats of a high-quality flat or satin-finish white paint to the entire frame except the back. An oil-base or plastic-base paint such as Varathane is preferable to a latex paint. Sand the first coat lightly with a very fine sandpaper (#220 or finer), and fill with water putty any holes or depressions missed initially.

When the second coat has had at least a couple of days to dry, the relief pieces may be mounted. Run a strip of masking tape around the front edge of the frame to keep it clean. Before mounting any pieces permanently, set them all in their correct position in the frame, using the spacer blocks described in Section I, Chapter 2. Blocks should be set and left between all pieces and all four walls of the relief. Not only will this "trial run" determine the number of blocks you will need, it will also reveal any minor adjustments in size that need to be made (although there should not be any!). In setting the pieces of any of the wooden puzzles in Section III, long strips of plywood (of the right thickness) are more useful than blocks for maintaining long straight spaces of continuous width.

Often, most of the unmounted pieces of the relief can be left in position while the rest are being marked, bored and set in their holes with glue. Following the procedure described in Section I, Chapter 2, mount each of the relief pieces, removing the blocks only after all the pieces in a row or area are mounted.

When all pieces are mounted and the glue dried (but before removing the masking tape), turn the relief over to affix the hanging wire. From the top of the frame, measure down along the back edges of each side framing wall about one third the total height. Make marks for screw holes at points half the thickness of the framing walls. It is best to bore starting holes for the round-

head screws you will be using. Drive the screws in t within ¼″ of the wood. Wrap an end of 50-lb.-test (o heavier) picture wire around one screw at least twice then twist the wire around itself several times. Stretch across the back taut and wrap it around the other scre in the same way. Finish driving both screws into th frame as far as they will go. If you use a tight wire, th relief will hang almost flat against the wall.

When the masking tape is removed, your relief finished and ready to hang. There is no way to colo stain, seal, varnish, wax, shellac or otherwise preserv the wood pieces of the relief without changing the natural character, but there is no real necessity to. Th wood has been selected principally for its color, texture patterns and other features, and any polishing or pre serving agent will cover up and defeat the origina reasons for your choices. Sunlight will eventuall change the color of the relief just as it does the color o floors and architectural woodwork, but this will be gradual and natural change.